Born in 1965

by

Kerry Butters.

Born in 1965

Millennium: 2nd millennium

Centuries: 19th century – **20th century** – 21st century

Decades: 1930s 1940s 1950s – **1960s** – 1970s 1980s 1990s

Years: 1962 1963 1964 – **1965** – 1966 1967 1968

1965 (MCMLXV) was a common year starting on Friday
(dominical letter C) of the Gregorian calendar, the 1965th year of
the Common Era (CE) and *Anno Domini* (AD) designations, the
965th year of the 2nd millennium, the 65th year of the
20th century, and the 6th year of the 1960s decade.

Contents

- 1 Events
- 2 Births
- 3 Deaths
- 4 Nobel Prizes
- 5 In the News

Events

January

- January 1 – Canadian ship SS *Catala* is driven onto the beach in Ocean Shores, Washington, stranding her.
- January 4 – U.S. President Lyndon B. Johnson proclaims his "Great Society" during his State of the Union address.
- January 9 – The Mirzapur Cadet College formally opens for academic activities in East Pakistan (now Bangladesh).
- January 14 – The Prime Minister of Northern Ireland and the Taoiseach of the Republic of Ireland meet for the first time in 43 years.
- January 19 – The unmanned *Gemini 2* is launched on a suborbital test of various spacecraft systems.
- January 20
    - Lyndon B. Johnson is sworn in for his own full term as U.S. President.
    - Indonesian President Sukarno announces the withdrawal of the Indonesian government from the United Nations.

- January 26 – Anti-Hindi agitations break out in India, because of which Hindi does not get "National Language" status and remains one of the 23 official languages of India.
- January 30 – The state funeral of Sir Winston Churchill takes place in London with the largest assembly of statesmen in the world until the 2005 funeral of Pope John Paul II.

February

- February 4 – Trofim Lysenko is removed from his post as director of the Institute of Genetics at the Academy of Sciences in the Soviet Union and Lysenkoist theories subjected to criticism as pseudoscience.
- February 6 – English footballer Sir Stanley Matthews plays his final First Division game, at the record age of 50 years and 5 days.
- February 12 – The African and Malagasy Common Organization (Organization Commune Africaine et Malgache; OCAM) is formed as successor to the Afro-Malagasy Union for Economic Cooperation (Union Africaine et Malgache de Cooperation Economique; UAMCE), formerly the African and Malagasy Union (Union Africaine et Malgache; UAM).
- February 15 – A new red and white maple leaf design is inaugurated as the flag of Canada, replacing the Union Flag and the Canadian Red Ensign.
- February 17 – Joan Rivers makes her Tonight Show debut.
- February 18 – The Gambia becomes independent from the United Kingdom.

- February 20
  - *Ranger 8* crashes into the Moon, after a successful mission of photographing possible landing sites for the Apollo program astronauts.
  - Suat Hayri Ürgüplü forms the new (interim) government of Turkey (29th government).
- February 21 – African-American Muslim minister and human rights activist Malcolm X is assassinated in New York City.
- February 22 – A new, revised, color production of Rodgers and Hammerstein's *Cinderella* airs on CBS. Lesley Ann Warren makes her TV debut in the title role. The show becomes an annual tradition.

The newly adopted Flag of Canada

Flag of the newly independent Gambia

March

- March 2
  - Vietnam War: Operation Rolling Thunder – The United States Air Force 2d Air Division, United States Navy

and Republic of Vietnam Air Force begin a 3½-year aerial bombardment campaign against North Vietnam.
  - The film of *The Sound of Music* premieres at the Rivoli Theater in New York City.
- March 7 – Bloody Sunday: Some 200 Alabama State Troopers attack 525 civil rights demonstrators in Selma, Alabama as they attempt to march to the state capitol of Montgomery.
- March 8 – Vietnam War: Some 3,500 United States Marines arrive in Da Nang, South Vietnam, becoming the first American ground combat troops in Vietnam.
- March 9 – The second attempt to march from Selma to Montgomery, Alabama, under the leadership of Martin Luther King, Jr., stops at the bridge that was the site of Bloody Sunday, to hold a prayer service and return to Selma, in obedience to a court restraining order. White supremacists beat up white Unitarian Universalist minister James J. Reeb later that day in Selma.
- March 10
  - An engagement is announced between Princess Margriet of the Netherlands and Pieter van Vollenhoven, who will become the first commoner and the first Dutchman to marry into the Dutch Royal Family.
  - Goldie, a London Zoo golden eagle, is recaptured 12 days after her escape.
- March 11 – White Unitarian Universalist minister James J. Reeb, beaten by White supremacists in Selma, Alabama on March 9 following the second march from Selma, dies in a hospital in Birmingham, Alabama.
- March 15 – President Lyndon B. Johnson makes his "We Shall Overcome" speech.

- March 16 – Police clash with 600 SNCC marchers in Montgomery, Alabama.
- March 17
  - In Montgomery, Alabama, 1,600 civil rights marchers demonstrate at the Courthouse.
  - In response to the events of March 7 and 9 in Selma, Alabama, President Lyndon B. Johnson sends a bill to Congress that forms the basis for the Voting Rights Act of 1965. It is passed by the Senate May 26, the House July 10, and signed into law by President Johnson August 6.
- March 18
  - Cosmonaut Alexey Leonov, leaving his spacecraft *Voskhod 2* for 12 minutes, becomes the first person to walk in space.
  - A United States federal judge rules that SCLC has the lawful right to march to Montgomery, Alabama to petition for 'redress of grievances'.
- March 19 – The wreck of the SS *Georgiana*, reputed to have been the most powerful Confederate cruiser ever built, is discovered off the Isle of Palms, South Carolina, by teenage diver E. Lee Spence, exactly 102 years after she was sunk with a million dollar cargo, while attempting to run past the Union blockade into Charleston.
- March 20
  - "Poupée de cire, poupée de son", sung by France Gall (music and lyrics by Serge Gainsbourg) wins the Eurovision Song Contest 1965 for Luxembourg.
  - The Indo-Pakistani War of 1965 begins.

- March 21
  - Ranger program: NASA launches *Ranger 9*, which is the last in a series of unmanned lunar space probes.
  - Martin Luther King, Jr. leads 3,200 civil rights activists in the third march from Selma, Alabama to the capitol in Montgomery.
- March 22 – Nicolae Ceaușescu becomes the first secretary of the Romanian Communist Party.
- March 23
  - Events of March 23, 1965: Large student demonstration in Morocco, joined by discontented masses, meets with violent police and military repression.
  - *Gemini 3*: NASA launches the United States' first 2-person crew (Gus Grissom, John Young) into Earth orbit.
  - The first issue of *The Vigilant* is published from Khartoum.
- March 25 – Martin Luther King, Jr. and 25,000 civil rights activists successfully end the 4-day march from Selma, Alabama, to the capitol in Montgomery.
- March 30
  - Funeral services are held for Detroit homemaker Viola Liuzzo, who was shot dead by 4 Klansmen as she drove marchers back to Selma at night after the civil rights march.
  - The second ODECA charter, signed on 12 December 1962, becomes effective.

April

- April 3 – The world's first space nuclear power reactor, *SNAP-10A*, is launched by the United States from Vandenberg AFB, California. The reactor operates for 43 days and remains in low Earth orbit.
- April 5 – At the 37th Academy Awards, *My Fair Lady* wins 8 Academy Awards, including Best Picture and Best Director. Rex Harrison wins an Oscar for Best Actor. *Mary Poppins* takes home 5 Oscars. Julie Andrews wins an Academy Award for Best Actress for her performance in the title role. Sherman Brothers receives 2 Oscars including Best Song, "Chim Chim Cher-ee".
- April 6
  - The Intelsat I ("Early Bird") communications satellite is launched. It becomes operational May 2 and is placed in commercial service in June.
  - The British Government announces the cancellation of the TSR-2 aircraft project.
- April 9
  - The West German parliament extends the statute of limitations on Nazi war crimes.
  - In Houston, the Harris County Domed Stadium (more commonly known as the Astrodome) opens.
  - Charlie Brown and the *Peanuts* Gang appear on the cover of *Time*.
- April 11 – The 1965 Palm Sunday tornado outbreak: An estimated 51 tornadoes (47 confirmed) hit in 6 Midwestern states, killing between 256 and 271 people and injuring some 1,500 more.

- April 14 – *In Cold Blood* killers Richard Hickock and Perry Smith, convicted of murdering 4 members of the Herbert Clutter family of Holcomb, Kansas, are executed by hanging at the Kansas State Penitentiary for Men in Lansing, Kansas.
- April 17 – The first Students for a Democratic Society march against the Vietnam War draws 25,000 protestors to Washington, D.C.
- April 18 – Consecration of Saint Clement of Ohrid Macedonian Orthodox Cathedral in Toronto, Canada.
- April 21 – The New York World's Fair in Flushing Meadows, New York, reopens.
- April 23 – The Pennine Way officially opens.
- April 24
  - The 1965 Yerevan demonstrations start in Yerevan, demanding recognition of the Armenian Genocide.
  - The bodies of Portuguese opposition politician Humberto Delgado and his secretary Arajaryr Moreira de Campos are found in a forest near Villanueva del Fresno, Spain (they were killed February 12).
  - In the Dominican Republic, officers and civilians loyal to deposed President Juan Bosch mutiny against the right-wing junta running the country, setting up a provisional government. Forces loyal to the deposed military-imposed government stage a countercoup the next day, and civil war breaks out, although the new government retains its hold on power.
- April 25 – Teenage sniper Michael Clark kills 3 and wounds others shooting at cars from a hilltop along Highway 101 just south of Orcutt, California. Sixteen-year-old Clark kills himself as police rush the hilltop.
-

- April 28
  - U.S. troops occupy the Dominican Republic.
  - Vietnam War: Prime Minister of Australia Robert Menzies announces that the country will substantially increase its number of troops in South Vietnam, supposedly at the request of the Saigon government (it is later revealed that Menzies had asked the leadership in Saigon to send the request at the behest of the Americans).
- April 29 – Australia announces that it is sending an infantry battalion to support the South Vietnam government.

May

- May 1
  - Bob Askin replaces Jack Renshaw as Premier of New South Wales.
  - The Battle of Dong-Yin occurs as a conflict between Taiwan and the People's Republic of China.
  - Liverpool wins the FA Cup Final, beating Leeds Utd 2–1.
- May 5 – Forty men burn their draft cards at the University of California, Berkeley, and a coffin is marched to the Berkeley Draft Board.
- May 6 – A tornado outbreak near the Twin Cities in Minnesota kills 13 and injures 683.
- May 7 – The U.S. Steel freighter SS *Cedarville* collides with the SS *Topdalsfjord* and sinks near the Mackinac Bridge, killing 25. 10 are rescued from the *Cedarville*, the 3rd largest lake ship to sink after its sister the SS *Carl D. Bradley*, and the SS *Edmund Fitzgerald*.

- May 9 – Pianist Vladimir Horowitz returns to the stage after a 12-year absence, performing a legendary concert in Carnegie Hall in New York.
- May 12
  - West Germany and Israel establish diplomatic relations.
  - The Italian liner SS *Michelangelo* enters service.
- May 13 – A West German court of appeals condemns the behavior of ex-defense minister Franz Josef Strauss during the Spiegel scandal.
- May 21 – The largest antiwar teach-in to date begins at Berkeley, California, attended by 30,000.
- May 22 –
  - Several hundred Vietnam War protesters in Berkeley, California, march to the Draft Board again to burn 19 more cards. Lyndon Johnson is hung in effigy.
  - The first skateboarding championship is held.
- May 25 – Muhammad Ali knocks out Sonny Liston in the first round of their championship rematch with the "Phantom Punch" at the Central Maine Civic Center in Lewiston.
- May 27 – Internazionale beats Benfica 1-0 at the San Siro, Milan and wins the 1964-65 European Cup (football).
- May 29 – A mining accident in Dhanbad, India kills 274.
- May 31 – Racing driver Jim Clark wins the Indianapolis 500, and later wins the Formula One world driving championship in the same year.

June

Green Library at Florida International University in Miami, FL

- June 1
  - Florida International University is founded in Miami.
  - A coal mine explosion in Fukuoka, Japan kills 237.
- June 2 – Vietnam War: The first contingent of Australian combat troops arrives in South Vietnam.
- June 3 – *Gemini 4*: Astronaut Edward Higgins White makes the first U.S. space walk.
- June 7 – Kakanj mine disaster: A mining accident in Kakanj, Bosnia and Herzegovina, results in 128 deaths.
- June 10 – Vietnam War – Battle of Dong Xoai: About 1,500 Viet Cong mount a mortar attack on Đồng Xoài, overrunning its military headquarters and the adjoining militia compound.
- June 16 – A planned anti-Vietnam War protest at The Pentagon becomes a teach-in, with demonstrators distributing 50,000 leaflets in and around the building.
- June 19 – Houari Boumediene's Revolutionary Council ousts Ahmed Ben Bella, in a bloodless coup in Algeria.
- June 20 – Police in Algiers break up demonstrations by people who have taken to the streets chanting slogans in support of deposed President Ahmed Ben Bella.

- June 22 – The Treaty on Basic Relations between Japan and the Republic of Korea is signed in Tokyo.
- June 25 – A U.S. Air Force Boeing C-135 Stratolifter bound for Okinawa crashes just after takeoff at MCAS El Toro in Orange County, California, killing all 85 on board.

July

- July – The Commonwealth secretariat is created.
- July 9 – Sonny & Cher release I Got You Babe which would go on to #1 in the US, UK & Canada and establish them as international icons.
- July 14 – U.S. spacecraft *Mariner 4* flies by Mars, becoming the first spacecraft to return images from the Red Planet.
- July 15 – Greek Prime minister Georgios Papandreou and his government are dismissed by King Constantine II.
- July 16 – The Mont Blanc Tunnel is inaugurated by presidents Giuseppe Saragat and Charles de Gaulle.
- July 24 – Vietnam War: Four F-4C Phantoms escorting a bombing raid at Kang Chi are targeted by antiaircraft missiles, in the first such attack against American planes in the war. One is shot down and the other 3 sustain damage.
- July 25 – Bob Dylan elicits controversy among folk purists by "going electric" at the Newport Folk Festival.
- July 26 – The Maldives receive full independence from Great Britain.
- July 27 – Edward Heath becomes Leader of the British Conservative Party.
- July 28 – Vietnam War: U.S. President Lyndon B. Johnson announces his order to increase the number of United States troops in South Vietnam from 75,000 to 125,000, and to more

than double the number of men drafted per month - from 17,000 to 35,000.
- July 29 – The Beatles second movie Help! premieres.
- July 30 – War on Poverty: U.S. President Lyndon B. Johnson signs the Social Security Act of 1965 into law, establishing Medicare and Medicaid.

August

- August 1 – Cigarette advertising is banned on British television.
- August 6 – U.S. President Lyndon B. Johnson signs the Voting Rights Act of 1965 into law.
- August 7 – Tunku Abdul Rahman, Prime Minister of Malaysia, recommends the expulsion of Singapore from the Federation of Malaysia, negotiating its separation with Lee Kuan Yew, Prime Minister of Singapore.
- August 9
  - Singapore is expelled from the Federation of Malaysia, which recognises it as a sovereign nation. Lee Kuan Yew announces Singapore's independence and assumes the position of Prime Minister of the new island nation – a position he holds until 1990.
  - An explosion at an Arkansas missile plant kills 53.
  - Indonesian president Sukarno collapses in public.
- August 11 – The Watts Riots begin in Los Angeles.
- August 13 – The rock group Jefferson Airplane debuts at the Matrix in San Francisco and begins to appear there regularly.
- August 15 – The Beatles perform the first stadium concert in the history of music, playing before 55,600 persons at Shea Stadium in New York City.

- August 18 – Vietnam War – Operation Starlite: 5,500 United States Marines destroy a Viet Cong stronghold on the Van Tuong peninsula in Quảng Ngãi Province, in the first major American ground battle of the war. The Marines were tipped-off by a Viet Cong deserter who said that there was an attack planned against the U.S. base at Chu Lai.
- August 19 – At the conclusion of the Frankfurt Auschwitz trials, 66 ex-SS personnel receive life sentences, 15 others smaller ones.
- August 20 – Jonathan Myrick Daniels, an Episcopal seminarian from Keene, New Hampshire, is murdered in Hayneville, Alabama while working in the African-American civil rights movement.
- August 21 – *Gemini 5* (Gordon Cooper, Pete Conrad) is launched on the first 1-week flight, as well as the first test of fuel cells for electrical power.
- August 30
  - Casey Stengel announces his retirement after 55 years in baseball.
  - Rock musician Bob Dylan releases his influential album *Highway 61 Revisited*, featuring the song "Like a Rolling Stone".
  - An avalanche buries a dam construction site at Saas-Fee, Switzerland, killing 90 workers.
- August 31 – President Johnson signs a law penalizing the burning of draft cards with up to 5 years in prison and a $1,000 fine.

September

- September 2 – Pakistani troops enter the Indian sector of Kashmir, while Indian troops try to invade Lahore.
- September 6 – The Islamic Republic of Pakistan observes its Defence Day, on account of successful defence of Lahore and other important areas against India.
- September 7
    - Pakistan celebrates Air Force Day on account of heavy retaliations to India.
    - The People's Republic of China announces that it will reinforce its troops on the Indian border.
    - Vietnam War: In a follow-up to August's Operation Starlite, United States Marines and South Vietnamese forces initiate Operation Piranha on the Batangan Peninsula, 23 miles (37 km) south of the Chu Lai Marine base.
- September 8
    - India opens 2 additional fronts against Pakistan.
    - The Pakistan Navy raids Indian coasts without any resistance in Operation Dwarka (Pakistan celebrates Victory Day annually).
    - Dorothy Dandridge dies of a drug overdose.
- September 9
    - Sandy Koufax of the Los Angeles Dodgers pitches a perfect game in a baseball match against the Chicago Cubs. The opposing pitcher, Bob Hendley, allows only 1 run, which is unearned, and only one hit, making this the lowest-hit game (1) in baseball history. It is Koufax's fourth no-hitter in as many seasons.

- U.N. Secretary General U Thant negotiates with Pakistan President Ayub Khan.
- U Thant recommends China for United Nations membership.
- Hurricane Betsy roars ashore near New Orleans with winds of 145 mph (233 km/h), causing 76 deaths and $1.42 billion in damage. The storm is the first hurricane to cause $1 billion in unadjusted damages, giving it the nickname "Billion Dollar Betsy". It is the last major hurricane to strike New Orleans until Hurricane Katrina 40 years later.
- September 13 – The Congress of Arab Countries begins in Casablanca; Habib Bourguiba of Tunisia boycotts the meeting.
- September 14
  - The fourth and final period of the Second Vatican Council opens.
  - The infamous "bad sitcom" My Mother The Car premieres on NBC.
- September 16
  - China protests against Indian provocations in its border region.
  - In Iraq, Prime Minister Arif Abd ar-Razzaq's attempted coup fails.
- September 17 – King Constantine II of Greece forms a new government with Prime Minister Stephanos Stephanopoulos, in an attempt to end a 2-year-old political crisis.
- September 18
  - In Denmark, Palle Sørensen shoots 4 policemen in pursuit; he is apprehended the same day.

- Comet Ikeya–Seki is first sighted by Japanese astronomers.
- Soviet Premier Alexei Kosygin invites the leaders of India and Pakistan to meet in the Soviet Union to negotiate.
- September 20 – Vietnam War: An USAF F-104 Starfighter piloted by Captain Philip Eldon Smith is shot down by a Chinese MiG-19 Farmer. The pilot is held until 15 March 1973.
- September 21 – Gambia, Maldives and Singapore are admitted as members of the United Nations.
- September 22 – Radio Peking announces that Indian troops have dismantled their equipment on the Chinese side of the border.
- September 24
  - Fighting resumes between Indian and Pakistani troops.
  - The British governor of Aden cancels the constitution and takes direct control of the protectorate, due to the bad security situation.
- September 25 – The *Tom & Jerry* cartoon series makes its world broadcast premiere on CBS.
- September 27 – The largest tanker ship at this time, *Tokyo Maru*, is launched in Yokohama, Japan.
- September 28
  - Fidel Castro announces that anyone who wants to can emigrate to the United States.
  - Taal Volcano in Luzon, Philippines, erupts, killing hundreds.

- September 30
  - The Indonesian army, led by General Suharto, crushes an alleged communist coup attempt (see Transition to the New Order and 30 September Movement).
  - The classic family sci-fi show *Thunderbirds* debuts on ITV in the U.K.

October

- October 3
  - Fidel Castro announces that Che Guevara has resigned and left the country.
  - U.S. President Lyndon B. Johnson signs the Immigration and Nationality Act of 1965 which ends quotas based on national origin.
- October 4
  - At least 150 killed when a commuter train derails at the outskirts of Durban, KwaZulu-Natal, South Africa.
  - Prime minister Ian Smith of Rhodesia and Arthur Bottomley of the Commonwealth of Nations begin negotiations in London.
  - Pope Paul VI visits the United States. He appears for a Mass in Yankee Stadium and makes a speech at the United Nations.
  - The University of California, Irvine opens its doors.
- October 5 – Pakistan severs diplomatic relations with Malaysia because of their disagreement in the UN.
- October 6 – Ian Brady, a 27-year-old stock clerk from Hyde in Cheshire, is arrested for allegedly hacking to death (with a hatchet) 17-year-old apprentice electrician Edward Evans at a house on the Hattersley housing estate.

- October 7 – Seven Japanese fishing boats are sunk off Guam by super typhoon Carmen; 209 are killed.
- October 8
  - Indonesian killings of 1965–66: The Indonesian army instigates the arrest and execution of communists which last until next March.
  - The 7 Fundamental Principles of the Red Cross and Red Crescent are adopted at the XX International Conference in Vienna, Austria.
  - The International Olympic Committee admits East Germany as a member.
  - The Post Office Tower opens in London.
- October 9
  - Yale University presents the *Vinland map*.
  - A brigade of South Korean soldiers arrive in South Vietnam.
- October 10 – The first group of Cuban refugees travels to the U.S.
- October 12
  - Per Borten forms a government in Norway.
  - The U.N. General Council recommends that the United Kingdom try everything to stop a rebellion in Rhodesia.
- October 13 – Congo President Joseph Kasavubu fires Prime Minister Moise Tshombe and forms a provisional government, with Évariste Kimba in a leading position.
- October 15 – Vietnam War: The Catholic Worker Movement stages an anti-war protest in Manhattan. One draft card burner is arrested, the first under the new law.
- October 16
  - Moors murders: Police find a girl's body on Saddleworth Moor near Oldham in Lancashire. The

body is quickly identified as that of 10-year-old Lesley Ann Downey, who disappeared on Boxing Day the previous year from a fairground in the Ancoats area of Manchester. Ian Brady, arrested for the murder of a 17-year-old man in nearby Hattersley, is charged with murdering Lesley, as is his 23-year-old girlfriend Myra Hindley.

- Anti-war protests draw 100,000 in 80 U.S. cities and around the world.

- October 17 – The New York World's Fair at Flushing Meadows, closes. Due to financial losses, some of the projected site park improvements fail to materialize.
- October 18 – The Indonesian government outlaws the Communist Party of Indonesia.
- October 20 – Ludwig Erhard is re-elected Chancellor of West Germany (he had first been elected in 1963).
- October 21
  - Comet Ikeya–Seki approaches perihelion, passing 450,000 kilometers from the sun.
  - The Organization of African Unity meets in Accra, Ghana.
- October 22
  - French authors André Figueras and Jacques Laurent are fined for their comments against Charles de Gaulle.
  - African countries demand that the United Kingdom use force to prevent Rhodesia from declaring unilateral independence.
  - Colonel Christophe Soglo stages a second coup in Dahomey.

- October 24
  - British Prime Minister Harold Wilson and Commonwealth Secretary Arthur Bottomley travel to Rhodesia for negotiations.
  - British police find the decomposed body of a boy on Saddleworth Moor.
- October 25 – The Soviet Union declares its support of African countries in case Rhodesia unilaterally declares independence.
- October 26
  - Anti-government demonstrations occur in the Dominican Republic.
  - Police discover the body of Sylvia Likens in Indianapolis.
- October 27
  - Brazilian president Humberto de Alencar Castelo Branco removes power from parliament, legal courts and opposition parties.
  - Süleyman Demirel of AP forms the new government of Turkey (30th government).

The Gateway Arch

- October 28
  - French Foreign Minister Maurice Couve de Murville travels to Moscow.
  - Pope Paul VI promulgates *Nostra aetate*, a "Declaration on the Relation of the (Roman Catholic) Church with Non-Christian Religions" by the Second Vatican Council which includes a statement that Jews are not collectively responsible for the death of Jesus (Jewish deicide).
  - In St. Louis, Missouri, the 630-foot (190 m)-tall inverted catenary steel Gateway Arch is completed.
  - Mehdi Ben Barka, a Moroccan politician, is kidnapped in Paris and never seen again.
- October 29
  - Moors murders: Ian Brady and Myra Hindley appear in court, charged with the murders of Edward Evans (17), Lesley Ann Downey (10), and John Kilbride (12) from Manchester.
  - An 80-kiloton nuclear device is detonated at Amchitka Island, Alaska as part of the Vela Uniform program, code-named Project Long Shot.
- October 30
  - Vietnam War: Near Da Nang, United States Marines repel an intense attack by Viet Cong forces, killing 56 guerrillas. A sketch of Marine positions is found on the dead body of a 13-year-old Vietnamese boy who sold drinks to the Marines the day before.
  - In Washington, D.C., a pro-Vietnam War march draws 25,000.

November

- November 1 – A trolleybus plunges into the Nile at Cairo, killing 74 passengers.
- November 2
    - Republican John Lindsay is elected mayor of New York City.
    - Quaker Norman Morrison, 32, sets himself on fire in front of The Pentagon.
- November 3 – French President Charles de Gaulle announces that he will stand for re-election.
- November 5 – Martial law is announced in Rhodesia. The United Nations General Assembly accepts British intent to use force against Rhodesia if necessary by a vote of 82–9.
- November 6 – Freedom Flights begin: Cuba and the United States formally agree to start an airlift for Cubans who want to go to the United States (by 1971 250,000 Cubans take advantage of this program).
- November 7 – Pillsbury's world-famous mascot, the Pillsbury Doughboy, is created.
- November 8
    - Vietnam War – Operation Hump: The 173rd Airborne is ambushed by over 1,200 Viet Cong.
    - The British Indian Ocean Territory is created, consisting of Chagos Archipelago, Aldabra, Farquhar and Desroches islands (on June 23, 1976 Aldabra, Farquhar and Des Roches are returned to the Seychelles).
    - The Murder (Abolition of Death Penalty) Act 1965 is given Royal Assent, suspending the death penalty for

murder in the United Kingdom; renewal of the Act in 1969 makes the abolition permanent.

- The soap opera *Days of Our Lives* debuts on NBC.
- November 9
    - Northeast blackout of 1965: Several U.S. states (VT, NH, MA, CT, RI, NY and portions of NJ) and parts of Canada are hit by a series of blackouts lasting up to 13½ hours.
    - Vietnam War: In New York City, 22-year-old Catholic Worker Movement member Roger Allen LaPorte sets himself on fire in front of the United Nations building in protest against the war.
- November 11
    - In Rhodesia (modern-day Zimbabwe), the white-minority government of Ian Smith unilaterally declares *de facto* independence ('UDI').
    - United Airlines Flight 227 a Boeing 727-22, crashes short of the runway and catches fire at Salt Lake City International Airport in Salt Lake City; 43 out of 91 passengers and crew perish.
- November 12 – A UN Security Council resolution (voted 10–0) recommends that other countries not recognize independent Rhodesia.
- November 13 – The SS *Yarmouth Castle* burns and sinks 60 miles (97 km) off Nassau, Bahamas, with the loss of 90 lives.
- November 14 – Vietnam War – Battle of Ia Drang: In the Ia Drang Valley of the Central Highlands in Vietnam, the first major engagement of the war between regular United States and North Vietnamese forces begins.
- November 15 – U.S. racer Craig Breedlove sets a new land speed record of 600.601 mph (966.574 km/h).

- November 16 – Venera program: The Soviet Union launches the *Venera 3* space probe from Baikonur, Kazakhstan toward Venus (on March 1, 1966 it becomes the first spacecraft to reach the surface of another planet).
- November 20 – The United Nations Security Council recommends that all states stop trading with Rhodesia.
- November 21 – Mireille Mathieu sings on France's Télé-Dimanche and begins her successful singing career (Dimanche is French for Sunday).
- November 22
  - *Man of La Mancha* opens in a Greenwich Village theatre in New York and eventually becomes one of the greatest musical hits of all time, winning a Tony Award for its star, Richard Kiley.
  - The United Nations Development Programme (UNDP) is established as a specialized agency of the United Nations.
- November 23 – Soviet general Mikhail Kazakov assumes command of the Warsaw Pact.
- November 24 – Congolese lieutenant general Mobutu ousts Joseph Kasavubu and declares himself president.
- November 26 – At the Hammaguir launch facility in the Sahara Desert, France launches a Diamant A rocket with its first satellite, *Asterix-1* on board, becoming the third country to enter outer space.
- November 27
  - Tens of thousands of Vietnam War protesters picket the White House, then march on the Washington Monument.
  - Vietnam War: The Pentagon tells U.S. President Lyndon B. Johnson that if planned major sweep

operations to neutralize Viet Cong forces during the next year are to succeed, the number of American troops in Vietnam will have to be increased from 120,000 to 400,000.

- November 28 – Vietnam War: In response to U.S. President Lyndon B. Johnson's call for "more flags" in Vietnam, Philippines President-elect Ferdinand Marcos announces he will send troops to help fight in South Vietnam.
- November 29 – The Canadian satellite *Alouette 2* is launched.

December

- December 1 – The Border Security Force is established in India as a special force to guard the borders.
- December 3
  - The first British aid flight arrives in Lusaka; Zambia had asked for British help against Rhodesia.
  - Members of the Organization of African Unity decide to sever diplomatic relations with the United Kingdom, unless the British Government ends the rebellion of Rhodesia by mid-December.
  - The Beatles release *Rubber Soul*.
- December 5
  - Charles de Gaulle is re-elected as French president with 10,828,421 votes.
  - The "Glasnost Meeting" in Moscow becomes the first spontaneous political demonstration, and the first demonstration for civil rights in the Soviet Union.

- December 8
  - Rhodesian prime minister Ian Smith warns that Rhodesia will resist a trade embargo by neighboring countries with force.
  - The Race Relations Act becomes the first legislation to address racial discrimination in the United Kingdom.
  - The Second Vatican Council closes.
- December 9 – *A Charlie Brown Christmas*, the first *Peanuts* television special, debuts on CBS, quickly becoming an annual tradition.
- December 15
  - The Caribbean Free Trade Association (CARIFTA) is formed.
  - Tanzania and Guinea sever diplomatic relations with the United Kingdom.
  - *Gemini 6* and *Gemini 7* perform the first controlled rendezvous in Earth orbit.
- December 17 – The British government begins an oil embargo against Rhodesia; the United States joins the effort.
- December 20 – The World Food Programme is made a permanent agency of the United Nations.
- December 21
  - The Soviet Union announces that it has shipped rockets to North Vietnam.
  - In West Germany, Konrad Adenauer resigns as chairman of the Christian Democratic Party.
  - The United Nations adopts the International Convention on the Elimination of All Forms of Racial Discrimination.
  - A new 1-hour German-American production of the ballet *The Nutcracker*, with an international cast that

includes Edward Villella in the title role, makes its U.S. television debut. It is repeated annually by CBS over the next 3 years but after that is virtually forgotten until issued on DVD in 2009 by Warner Archive.

- December 22
    - Military coup occurs in Dahomey.
    - A 70 mph (110 km/h) speed limit is imposed on British roads.
    - David Lean's film of *Doctor Zhivago*, starring Omar Sharif and Julie Christie, is released.
- December 25 – The Yemeni Nasserist Unionist People's Organisation is founded in Ta'izz.
- December 27 – The British oil platform *Sea Gem* collapses in the North Sea.
- December 28 – Italian Foreign Minister Amintore Fanfani resigns.
- December 30
    - President Kenneth Kaunda of Zambia announces that Zambia and the United Kingdom have agreed on a deadline before which the Rhodesian white government should be ousted.
    - Ferdinand Marcos becomes President of the Philippines.
- December 31 – Bokassa takes power in the Central African Republic.

Date unknown

- Tokyo officially becomes the largest city of the world, taking the lead from New York City.
- The Council for National Academic Awards is established in the UK.
- TAT-4 cable goes into operation.
- Aborigines are given the vote in Queensland.

Births

January

Julia Ormond

James Nesbitt

Sophie, Countess of Wessex

- January 4
  - Beth Gibbons, English singer, lead singer of the band Portishead
  - Julia Ormond, British actress
  - Aditya Pancholi, Indian actor
- January 5
  - Vinnie Jones, British footballer-turned-actor
  - Patrik Sjöberg, Swedish high jumper
- January 6 – Konnan, Cuban-born professional wrestler
- January 9
  - Haddaway, German singer
  - Farah Khan, Indian choreographer, film director
  - Joely Richardson, British actress
  -

- January 12
  - Nikolai Borschevsky, Russian professional ice hockey player (retired)
  - Maybrit Illner, German television journalist and presenter
  - Rob Zombie, American musician
- January 14
  - Shamil Basayev, Chechen terrorist (d. 2006)
  - Marc Delissen, Dutch field hockey player
  - Bob Essensa, Canadian ice hockey player
  - Hugh Fearnley-Whittingstall, British chef
- January 15 – James Nesbitt, Northern Irish actor
- January 18
  - Dave Attell, American comedian
  - Paudge Behan, Irish actor
- January 20 – Sophie, Countess of Wessex, wife of Prince Edward, Earl of Wessex
- January 21 – Jam Master Jay, American DJ, rapper and producer (d. 2002)
- January 22
  - DJ Jazzy Jeff, African-American rapper and actor
  - Diane Lane, American actress
- January 24 – Mike Awesome, American professional wrestler (d. 2007)
- January 25 – Esa Tikkanen, Finnish ice hockey player
- January 26 – Natalia Yurchenko, Soviet gymnast
- January 27
  - Alan Cumming, Scottish actor
  - Ignacio Noé, Argentine artist
- January 29 – Dominik Hašek, Czech hockey player

February

Chris Rock

Michael Bay

Dr. Dre

- February 1
  - Brandon Lee, Chinese-American actor (d. 1993)
  - Sherilyn Fenn, American actress
  - Princess Stéphanie of Monaco
- February 3
  - Mattanya Cohen, Israeli diplomat
  - Maura Tierney, American actress

- February 4 – Jerome Brown, American football player (d. 1992)
- February 5 – Gheorghe Hagi, Romanian footballer
- February 7 – Chris Rock, African-American actor and comedian
- February 8 – Dicky Cheung, Hong Kong actor
- February 11 – Stephen Gregory, American actor
- February 17– Michael Bay, American film director
- February 18 – Dr. Dre, African-American rapper and music producer
- February 22 – Dean Karr, American director and photographer
- February 23
  - Kristin Davis, American actress
  - Michael Dell, American computer manufacturer
- February 25 – Sylvie Guillem, French ballerina
- February 27 – Joakim Sundström, Swedish sound editor, sound designer and musician
- February 28 – Park Gok-ji, South Korean film editor

March

Sarah Jessica Parker

Aamir Khan

- March 1
    - Stewart Elliott, Canadian jockey
    - Booker Huffman, American professional wrestler, 5-time WCW World Champion
- March 3 – Dragan Stojković, Serbian footballer and coach
- March 4
    - Paul W. S. Anderson, British filmmaker, producer and screenwriter
    - Ron Gant, American baseball player
    - Jonathan Shearer, Scottish castaway
    - WestBam, German rave techno DJ
- March 7 – Jesper Parnevik, Swedish golfer
- March 8 – Kenny Smith, American basketball player
- March 9 – Benito Santiago, American baseball player
- March 9 – Mike Pollock, American voice actor
- March 10 – Rod Woodson, American football player
- March 11
    - Jesse Jackson, Jr., African-American politician
    - Laurence Llewelyn-Bowen, British designer and television presenter
    - Andy Sturmer, American musician (Jellyfish)
- March 12
    - Steve Finley, American baseball player

- o Liza Umarova, Chechen singer and actress
- March 14
  - o Kevin Brown, American baseball player
  - o Aamir Khan, Indian Bollywood actor, film director, producer, film editor and script writer
- March 19 – Joseph D. Kucan, American video game developer
- March 20 – Taeko Kawata, Japanese voice actress
- March 21 – Wakana Yamazaki, Japanese voice actress
- March 23 – Marti Pellow, Scottish singer (Wet Wet Wet)
- March 24 – The Undertaker, American professional wrestler ("The Undertaker")
- March 25
  - o Avery Johnson, American basketball player and coach
  - o Stefka Kostadinova, Bulgarian high jumper and president of the Bulgarian Olympic Committee
  - o Sarah Jessica Parker, American actress
- March 27 – Francisco Ribeiro, Portuguese musician and composer (Madredeus) (d. 2010)
- March 29 – Voula Patoulidou, Greek athlete
- March 30 – Piers Morgan, British journalist and television personality

April

Robert Downey Jr.

Jon Cryer

Martin Lawrence

Kevin James

- April 1
  - Bekir Bozdağ, Turkish theologian, lawyer, and politician
  - Mark Jackson, American basketball coach
- April 2 – Rodney King, African-American victim of police brutality (d. 2012)
- April 3
  - Julie Anne Haddock, American actress
  - Nazia Hassan, Pakistani pop singer (d. 2000)
- April 4 – Robert Downey Jr., American actor

- April 6
    - Frank Black, American musician
    - Rica Reinisch, German swimmer
- April 7 – Bill Bellamy, American actor and comedian
- April 9 – Paulina Porizkova, Swedish-American model and actress
- April 11 – Eelco van Asperen, Dutch computer scientist
- April 12 – Tom O'Brien, American actor-producer
- April 13
    - Patricio Pouchulu, Argentine architect
    - The Real Darren Stevens, Canadian radio personality
- April 15 – Linda Perry, American musician
- April 16
    - Jon Cryer, American actor
    - Martin Lawrence, African-American actor, comedian, and producer
- April 18 – Wil Johnson, English actor
- April 19 – Suge Knight, African-American record producer
- April 23 – Tommy DeCarlo, American singer and songwriter
- April 26
    - Kevin James, American comedian and actor

May

John C. Reilly

Brooke Shields

- May 3 – Gary Mitchell, Irish playwright
- May 4 – Aykut Kocaman, Turkish footballer
- May 7
  - Owen Hart, Canadian professional wrestler (d. 1999)
  - Norman Whiteside, Northern Irish football player
- May 9 – Steve Yzerman, Canadian hockey player
- May 10
  - Linda Evangelista, Canadian supermodel
  - Kiyoyuki Yanada, Japanese voice actor
- May 11
  - Monsour del Rosario, Filipino Olympic athlete and actor
- May 12 – Renée Simonsen, Danish model and writer
- May 13
  - Tim Chapman, American bounty hunter
  - José Antonio Delgado, Venezuelan mountain climber (d. 2006)
  - Hikari Ōta, Japanese comedian
- May 14 – Eoin Colfer, Irish novelist
- May 16 – Krist Novoselic, American rock bassist (Nirvana)
- May 17 – Trent Reznor, American rock musician (Nine Inch Nails)
- May 19 – Philippe Dhondt, French singer known as Boris

- May 23
  - Manuel Sanchís Hontiyuelo, Spanish footballer
  - Kappei Yamaguchi, Japanese voice actor
- May 24
  - Carlos Franco, Paraguayan golfer
  - John C. Reilly, American actor
  - Shinichirō Watanabe, Japanese anime director
- May 25 – Yahya Jammeh, President of the Gambia
- May 27 – Todd Bridges, African-American actor
- May 31
  - Brooke Shields, American actress and supermodel
  - Yoko Soumi, Japanese voice actress

June

- June 1
  - Larisa Lazutina, Russian cross-country skier
  - Nigel Short, English chess player
- June 2 – Steve and Mark Waugh, Australian cricketers
- June 4 – Mick Doohan, Australian motorcycle racer
- June 6
  - Cam Neely, Canadian ice hockey player
  - Megumi Ogata, Japanese voice actress and singer
- June 7
  - Mick Foley, American professional wrestler
  - Jean-Pierre François, French footballer and singer
  - Damien Hirst, British artist
  - Christine Roque, French singer
- June 8
  - Chris Chavis ("Tatanka"), American professional wrestler
  - Kevin Ritz, American former MLB pitcher

- June 10
    - Veronica Ferres, German actress
    - Scott Graham, American sportscaster
    - Elizabeth Hurley, English model and actress
- June 11 – Manuel Uribe, morbidly obese Mexican (d. 2014)
- June 15 – Bernard Hopkins, American boxer
- June 17
    - Dan Jansen, American speedskater
    - Dara O'Kearney, Irish ultra runner and professional poker player
- June 23 – Paul Arthurs, British rock guitarist (Oasis)
- June 26 – Mike Breen, American sports announcer
- June 27 – Ashley Richardson, American model
- June 28
    - Belayneh Dinsamo, Ethiopian long-distance runner
    - Sonny Strait, American voice actor
- June 29 – Matthew Weiner, American writer, director, and producer of television drama

July

Slash

Jeremy Piven

Stuart Scott

J. K. Rowling

- July 1 – Harald Zwart, Norwegian film director
- July 3
  - Shinya Hashimoto, Japanese professional wrestler (d. 2005)
  - Connie Nielsen, Danish actress
- July 4
  - Horace Grant, American basketball player
  - Jo Whiley, British radio DJ

- July 5
  - Kathryn Erbe, American actress
  - Eyran Katsenelenbogen, Israeli jazz pianist
- July 11 – Ernesto Hoost, Dutch kickboxer
- July 17
  - Ken Evraire, Canadian television journalist, host and former professional football league player with Hamilton Tiger Cats
  - Martin Kelly (Heavenly), British musician, music manager, record label boss, music publisher and author
  - Craig Morgan, American country music artist
  - Santiago Segura, Spanish actor, screenwriter, producer and director
  - Alex Winter, American actor
- July 19
  - Dame Evelyn Glennie, Scottish virtuoso percussionist
  - Stuart Scott, American sports reporter and ESPN anchor (d. 2015)
- July 21 – Guðni Bergsson, Icelandic footballer
- July 22 – Shawn Michaels, American professional wrestler
- July 23 – Slash (Saul Hudson), American rock musician (Guns N' Roses)
- July 24 – Brian Blades, American National Football League wide receiver
- July 25 – Steven Weil, Orthodox Union Executive Vice-President
- July 26
  - Vladimir Cruz, Cuban actor
  - Jeremy Piven, American actor
- July 27
  - José Luis Chilavert, Paraguayan footballer

- ○ Trifon Ivanov, Bulgarian footballer (d. 2016)
- July 31 – J. K. Rowling, English author

August

Sam Mendes

Kyra Sedgwick

- August 1 – Sam Mendes, English film director
- August 2
  - ○ Sandra Ng, Hong Kong actress
  - ○ Hisanobu Watanabe, Japanese baseball player and coach
- August 4
  - ○ Dennis Lehane, American crime writer
  - ○ Fredrik Reinfeldt, Swedish Prime Minister
  - ○

- August 6
  - David Robinson, American basketball player
  - Mark Speight, British television presenter (d. 2008)
- August 9 – Chin Ka-lok, Hong Kong actor
- August 10
  - Claudia Christian, American actress, writer, singer, musician, and director
  - Mike E. Smith, American jockey
  - John Starks, American basketball player
- August 11
  - Viola Davis, African-American actress
  - Duane Martin, American actor
- August 14
  - Emmanuelle Béart, French actress
  - Terry Richardson, American fashion photographer
- August 15
  - Vincent Kuk, Hong Kong director and actor
  - Mark Labbett, British mathematician
- August 18
  - Kōji Kikkawa, Japanese singer
  - Ikue Ōtani, Japanese voice actress
- August 19 – Kyra Sedgwick, American actress
- August 25 – Mia Zapata, American singer (d. 1993)
- August 28
  - Satoshi Tajiri, Japanese video game designer and *Pokémon* creator
  - Amanda Tapping, Canadian actress
  - Shania Twain, Canadian country singer and songwriter
- August 30 – Peter Grant, Scottish football player and manager

September

Charlie Sheen

Bashar al-Assad

Dmitry Medvedev

Petro Poroshenko

- September 1 – Craig McLachlan, Australian actor and singer
- September 2 – Lennox Lewis, British boxer
- September 3 – Charlie Sheen, American actor
- September 4 – Bowie Lam, Hong Kong actor and singer
- September 7 – Jörg Pilawa, German television presenter
- September 9
    - Dan Majerle, American basketball player
    - Constance Marie, American actress
- September 10 – Marco Pastors, Dutch politician
- September 11
    - Bashar al-Assad, President of Syria
    - Paul Heyman, American wrestling promoter, ECW
    - Moby, American musician
- September 12 – Einstein Kristiansen, Norwegian cartoonist, designer and TV host
- September 14
    - Dmitry Medvedev, President of Russia
    - Ron Pearson, American actor, comedian and juggler
- September 16 – Katy Kurtzman, American actress, director, and producer
- September 17 – Kyle Chandler, American actor
- September 19
    - Sabine Paturel, French singer
    - Tshering Tobgay, Prime Minister of Bhutan
- September 20 – Robert Rusler, American actor
- September 21
    - Cheryl Hines, American actress
    - Johanna Vuoksenmaa, Finnish film director
    - David Wenham, Australian actor
- September 25
    - Saffron Henderson, Canadian voice actress and singer

- o Scottie Pippen, American basketball player
- September 26
  - o Alexandra Lencastre, Portuguese actress
  - o Petro Poroshenko, President of Ukraine
- September 27
  - o Steve Kerr, American basketball player
  - o Peter MacKay, Canadian politician
- September 30 – Kathleen Madigan, American comedian

October

Steve Coogan

Stephen Tompkinson

Judge Jules

- October 1
  - Andreas Keller, German field hockey player
  - Cliff Ronning, Canadian ice hockey player
- October 3 – Jan-Ove Waldner, Swedish table tennis player
- October 4
  - John Melendez, American television announcer
  - Michiko Neya, Japanese voice actress
  - Rykers Solomon, Nauruan politician
  - Micky Ward, American boxer
- October 5
  - Mario Lemieux, Canadian ice hockey player
  - Patrick Roy, Canadian ice hockey player
- October 7 – Kumiko Watanabe, Japanese voice actress
- October 9 – Dionicio Cerón, Mexican long-distance runner
- October 10 – Chris Penn, American actor (d. 2006)
- October 11 – Ronit Roy, Indian film and television actor
- October 13 – Kalpana, Indian film actress (d. 2016)
- October 14
  - Steve Coogan, British comedian and actor
  - Constantine Koukias, Australian composer
- October 15 – Stephen Tompkinson, English actor
- October 16
  - Kang Kyung-ok, South Korean artist

- o Steve Lamacq, British radio DJ
- October 17 – Aravinda de Silva, Sri Lankan cricketer
- October 18
  - o Zakir Naik, Indian Islamic speaker and doctor
  - o Curtis Stigers, American jazz vocalist and saxophonist
- October 19 – Ty Pennington, American television presenter
- October 20 – Mikhail Shtalenkov, Russian ice hockey player
- October 26
  - o Aaron Kwok, Hong Kong singer and actor
  - o Julius O'Riordan, British dance music DJ, producer and entertainment lawyer
  - o Sakari Oramo, Finland Conductor and violinist
  - o Kelly Rowan, Canadian actress
  - o Kenneth Rutherford, New Zealand cricketer
- October 29 – Christy Clark, Canadian politician

November

Björk

Ben Stiller

Shahrukh Khan

- November 1 – Mia Korf, American actress
- November 2 – Shahrukh Khan, Indian actor, film/television producer and television presenter
- November 3 – Ann Scott, French novelist
- November 4
    - Wayne Static, American singer (Static-X) (d. 2014)
    - Kiersten Warren, American actress
- November 5
    - Famke Janssen, Dutch actress
    - Agnese Nano, Italian actress
- November 6 – Greg Graffin, American rock singer (Bad Religion)
- November 7
    - Sigrun Wodars, German athlete
    - Steve Parkin, English former footballer and manager
- November 9 – Bryn Terfel, Welsh baritone
- November 10 – Eddie Irvine, Northern Irish racecar driver
- November 13 – Rick Roberts, Canadian actor
- November 16 – Walter Stern, English music video and film director
- November 19
    - Paulo Barreto, Brazilian cryptographer

- Laurent Blanc, French football player and manager
- November 20
    - Michael Diamond, American rapper (Beastie Boys)
    - Yoshiki Hayashi, Japanese rock composer, piano and drummer (X Japan)
    - Takeshi Kusao, Japanese voice actor
- November 21
    - Björk, Icelandic singer-songwriter and musician
    - Alexander Siddig, Sudanese-born English actor
    - Yuriko Yamaguchi, Japanese voice actress
- November 22 – Mads Mikkelsen, Danish actor
- November 23
    - Don Frye, American professional wrestler and mixed martial arts fighter
    - Radion Gataullin, Uzbek-born, Russian pole-vaulter
- November 25 – Cris Carter, American football player
- November 28 – Peter Beagrie, English footballer
- November 30
    - Ben Stiller, American actor
    - Tashi Tenzing, Indian mountaineer

December

Katarina Witt

Andy Dick

Gong Li

Salman Khan

- December 3
    - Steve Harris, American actor
    - Katarina Witt, German figure skater
- December 4 – Anthony DeSando, American actor
- December 5
    - Carlton Palmer, English footballer
    - Johnny Rzeznik, American rock singer and guitarist (Goo Goo Dolls)

- December 7 – Teruyuki Kagawa, Japanese actor
- December 8 – Carina Lau Kar-ling, Chinese actress
- December 10 – Greg Giraldo, American comedian (d. 2010)
- December 14
  - Craig Biggio, American baseball player
  - Ted Raimi, American Actor, Producer and writer
- December 15
  - Luis Fabián Artime, Argentine footballer
  - Ted Slampyak, American comic strip cartoonist (Little Orphan Annie)
- December 18 – John Moshoeu, South African footballer
- December 19 – Jessica Steen, Canadian actress
- December 21
  - Andy Dick, American actor
  - Anke Engelke, German comedian, actress and voice-over actress
- December 22 – Lee Berger American-born explorer and paleoanthropologist
- December 27 – Salman Khan, Indian actor, television presenter
- December 28 – Allar Levandi, Estonian Nordic combined skier
- December 30
  - Heidi Fleiss, American madam
  - Zoe Kelli Simon, American actress
- December 31
  - Nicholas Sparks, American author
  - Gong Li, Chinese actress

Date unknown

- Niko Barun, Croatian artist

- Lauren Child, American author
- Jeffrey Colwell, American lawyer
- Antonio Helguera, Mexican cartoonist
- Bradley Joseph, American composer, pianist and keyboardist
- John Parry, American football official
- Paul Seawright, Irish photographer

Deaths

January

Winston Churchill

- January 4 – T. S. Eliot, American-born writer, Nobel Prize laureate (b. 1888)
- January 10 – Frederick Fleet, English sailor and lookout aboard the RMS *Titanic* (b. 1887)
- January 12 – Lorraine Hansberry, American writer (b. 1930)
- January 14 – Jeanette MacDonald, American actress and singer (b. 1903)
- January 20 – Alan Freed, American disc jockey (b. 1922)
- January 24 – Winston Churchill, Prime Minister of the United Kingdom, recipient of the Nobel Prize in Literature (b. 1874)

- January 27 – Abraham Walkowitz, American painter (b. 1878)
- January 28
  - Tich Freeman, English cricketer (b. 1888)
  - Maxime Weygand, French general (b. 1867)

February

Malcolm X

Stan Laurel

- February 5 – Irving Bacon, American actor (b. 1893)
- February 7 – Nance O'Neil, stage & film actress, friend of Lizzie Borden (b. 1874)
- February 9 – Khan Bahadur Ahsanullah, great Educationist, Philosopher, Philanthropist, Social Reformer, Sufi Thinker, Scientist and Spiritual Person, friend of A. K. Fazlul Huq (b. 1874)
- February 10 – Arthur C. Davis, American admiral (b. 1893)

- February 11 – Loyal Blaine Aldrich, American astronomer (b. 1884)
- February 13 – Gloria Morgan Vanderbilt, Swiss-born socialite (b. 1906)
- February 15 – Nat King Cole, American singer and musician (b. 1919)
- February 19 – Forrest Taylor, American stage, film and television actor (b. 1883)
- February 21 – Malcolm X, American activist (assassinated) (b. 1925)
- February 22 – Felix Frankfurter, U.S. Supreme Court Justice (b. 1882)
- February 23 – Stan Laurel, British actor (b. 1890)
- February 26 – George Adamski, Polish-born alleged UFO traveler (b. 1891)
- February 28 – Adolf Schärf, former President of Austria (b. 1890)

March

Farouk of Egypt

Princess Mary

- March 6 – Margaret Dumont, American actress (b. 1889)
- March 7 – Louise Mountbatten, Queen of Sweden and second wife of King Gustaf VI Adolf (b. 1889)
- March 13
  - Corrado Gini, Italian statistician (b. 1884)
  - Fan S. Noli, Albanian bishop, poet, and political figure (b. 1882)
- March 17
  - Nancy Cunard, English writer, heiress and political activist (b. 1896)
  - Amos Alonzo Stagg, American baseball, basketball, and football player and coach (b. 1862)
- March 18
  - King Farouk of Egypt (b. 1920)
  - Jack Quinlan, American Chicago Cubs radio broadcaster (b. 1927)
- March 23 – Mae Murray, stage & silent screen star (b. 1889)
- March 28
  - Richard Beesly, British Olympic gold medal-winning rower (b. 1907)
  - Mary, Princess Royal and Countess of Harewood (b. 1897)
  - Jack Hoxie, American actor, rodeo performer (b. 1885)

- March 30 – Philip Showalter Hench, American physician, recipient of the Nobel Prize in Physiology or Medicine (b. 1896)

April

- April 3
  - Ray Enright, American film director (b. 1896)
  - Ernst Kirchweger, Austrian communist and resistance fighter (b. 1897 or 1898)
- April 6 – William M. Branham, American Christian minister (b. 1909)
- April 8 – Lars Hanson, Swedish actor (b. 1886)
- April 10 – Linda Darnell, American actress (b. 1923)
- April 14 – Perry Smith (b. 1928) and Dick Hickock (b. 1931), American murderers of the Clutters in 1959 (executed)
- April 16 – Sydney Chaplin, American actor (b. 1885)
- April 18 – Guillermo González Camarena, Mexican inventor (b. 1917)
- April 21 – Edward Victor Appleton, English physicist, Nobel Prize laureate (b. 1892)
- April 24
  - Louise Dresser, American actress (b. 1878)
  - Owney Madden, English-born gangster (b. 1891)
- April 27 – Edward R. Murrow, American journalist (b. 1908)
- April 30 – Helen Chandler, American actress (b. 1906)

May

- May 1 – Spike Jones, American musician and bandleader (b. 1911)
- May 7 – Charles Sheeler, American photographer (b. 1883)

- May 9 – Leopold Figl, former Chancellor of Austria (b. 1902)
- May 10 – Hubertus van Mook, Acting Governor-General of the Dutch East Indies from 1942 to 1948 (b. 1894)
- May 14 – Frances Perkins, First woman appointed as a United States Presidential cabinet member (Labor) (b. 1880)
- May 18 – Eli Cohen, Israeli spy (b. 1924)
- May 22 – Christopher Stone, first disc jockey in the United Kingdom (b. 1882)
- May 23
  - David Smith, American sculptor (b. 1906)
  - Earl Webb, American baseball player (b. 1897)
- May 25 – Sonny Boy Williamson, American blues musician (b. 1899)

June

- June 1 – Curly Lambeau, American football coach (Green Bay Packers) and a member of the Pro Football Hall of Fame (b. 1898)
- June 7 – Judy Holliday, American actress (b. 1921)
- June 13 – Martin Buber, Austrian-Israeli philosopher (b. 1878)
- June 14 – H. V. Kaltenborn, American radio commentator (b. 1878)
- June 15
  - Steve Cochran, American actor (b. 1917)
  - Bill Gardner, American law enforcement agent and one of Eliot Ness's Untouchables (b. 1884)
  - E. A. Speiser, American Bible scholar (b. 1902)
- June 20 – Bernard Baruch, financier and presidential adviser (b. 1870)

- June 22 – David O. Selznick, American film producer (b. 1902)
- June 23 – Mary Boland, veteran stage & screen actress (b. 1880)
- June 24 – Kenneth Macdonald Beaumont, English legal pioneer (b. 1884)
- June 25 – Burr Shafer, American cartoonist (b. 1899)
- June 26 – Reginald Beckwith, English actor (b. 1908)
- June 28 – Red Nichols, American jazz cornettist (b. 1905)
- June 30 – Bessie Barriscale, American actress (b. 1884)

July

Syngman Rhee

- July 1 – Wally Hammond, English cricketer (b. 1903)
- July 7 – Moshe Sharett, second Prime Minister of Israel (b. 1894)
- July 14
  - Adlai Stevenson, American politician (b. 1900)
  - Max Woosnam, English sportsman (b. 1892)
- July 19
  - Clyde Beatty, American animal trainer (b. 1903)
  - Syngman Rhee, First President of South Korea (b. 1875)
- July 24 – Constance Bennett, American actress (b. 1904)

- July 25 – Freddie Mills, British boxing champion (b. 1919).
- July 28 – Rampo Edogawa, Japanese author and critic (b. 1894)
- July 30 – Jun'ichirō Tanizaki, Japanese writer (b. 1886)

August

Le Corbusier

- August 6
  - Nancy Carroll, American actress (b. 1903)
  - Everett Sloane, American actor (b. 1909)
- August 8 – Shirley Jackson, American author (b. 1916)
- August 9 – Creighton Hale, American actor (b. 1882)
- August 13 – Hayato Ikeda, former Prime Minister of Japan (b. 1899)
- August 25 – Moonlight Graham, American baseball player (b. 1879)
- August 27 – Le Corbusier, Swiss architect (b. 1887)
- August 28 – Giulio Racah, Israeli physicist (b. 1909)
- August 29 – Paul Waner, American baseball player (Pittsburgh Pirates) and a member of the MLB Hall of Fame (b. 1903)

September

- September 4
  - Alfred Bossom, English architect and politician (b. 1881)
  - Albert Schweitzer, Alsatian physician and missionary, recipient of the Nobel Peace Prize (b. 1875)
- September 8
  - Dorothy Dandridge, American actress (b. 1922)
  - Hermann Staudinger, German chemist, Nobel Prize laureate (b. 1881)
- September 10 – Bobby Jordan, American actor (b. 1923)
- September 12 – Lucian Truscott, American general (b. 1895)
- September 14 – J. W. Hearne, English cricketer (b. 1891)
- September 15 – Steve Brown, American musician (b. 1890)
- September 16 – Fred Quimby, American animated film producer (b. 1886)
- September 25 – Henry Hugh Tudor, British general (b. 1871)
- September 27
  - Clara Bow, American silent film actress (b. 1905)
  - Sir William Stanier, English steam locomotive engineer (London, Midland and Scottish Railway) (b. 1876)

October

- October 1 – Gareth Hughes, Welsh actor (b. 1894)
- October 3 – Zachary Scott, American actor (b. 1914)
- October 6 – Edward Evans, Murder victim (b. 1948)
- October 11
  - Dorothea Lange, American photographer (b. 1895)
  - Walther Stampfli, member of the Swiss Federal Council (b. 1884)

- October 12 – Paul Hermann Müller, Swiss chemist, recipient of the Nobel Prize in Physiology or Medicine (b. 1899)
- October 14 – Randall Jarrell, American poet (b. 1914)
- October 15 – Abraham Fraenkel, Israeli mathematician and recipient of the Israel Prize (b. 1891)
- October 17 – John Barton King, American cricketer (b. 1873)
- October 18 – Henry Travers, English actor (b. 1874)
- October 21 – Marie McDonald, American actress (b. 1923)
- October 22 – Paul Tillich, German American Christian existentialist philosopher and theologian (b. 1886)
- October 26 – Sylvia Likens, American murder victim (b. 1949)
- October 29
  - Miller Anderson, American Olympic diver (b. 1922)
  - Bill McKechnie, American baseball manager (Cincinnati Reds) and a member of the MLB Hall of Fame (b. 1886)
- October 30 – Arthur M. Schlesinger, Sr., American historian (b. 1888)
- October 31 – Rita Johnson, American actress (b. 1913)

November

- November 2 – Shah Rukh Khan, a Bollywood actor
- November 3 – William Leo Hansberry, African American Scholar and Uncle of Playwright Lorraine Hansberry (b. 1894)
- November 4 – Dickey Chapelle, American photojournalist (killed in action) (b. 1919)
- November 6
  - Edgard Varèse, French-born composer (b. 1883)
  - Clarence Williams, American musician (b. 1893)

- November 7 – Mirza Basheer-ud-Din Mahmood Ahmad, 2nd Caliph of Ahmadiyya Muslim Community in Islam (b. 1889)
- November 8 – Dorothy Kilgallen, American newspaper columnist (b. 1913)
- November 12 – Syedna Taher Saifuddin, Indian Bohra spiritual leader (b. 1888)
- November 16
    - Harry Blackstone, Sr., American magician (b. 1885)
    - W. T. Cosgrave, Irish politician (b. 1880)
- November 18 – Henry A. Wallace, Vice President of the United States (b. 1888)
- November 24 – Abdullah III Al-Salim Al-Sabah, Emir of Kuwait (b. 1895)
- November 25 – Dame Myra Hess, English pianist (b. 1890)

December

Somerset Maugham

- December 5 – Joseph Erlanger, Nobel Prize laureate (b. 1874)
- December 9 – Charles Hurlbut "Dutch" Sterrett, American professional baseball player (b. 1889)
- December 16 – W. Somerset Maugham, English writer (b. 1874)

- December 22
  - Richard Dimbleby, English broadcaster (b. 1913)
  - Al Ritz, American actor (b. 1901)
- December 24
  - John Black, English chairman of Standard-Triumph (b. 1895)
  - William M. Branham, American minister (b. 1909)
- December 29
  - Frank S. Nugent, American journalist (b. 1908)
  - Kosaku Yamada, Japanese composer and conductor (b. 1886)

Nobel Prizes

- Physics – Sin-Itiro Tomonaga, Julian Schwinger, Richard P. Feynman
- Chemistry – Robert Burns Woodward
- Physiology or Medicine – François Jacob, André Michel Lwoff, Jacques Monod
- Literature – Michail Aleksandrovich Sholokhov
- Peace – United Nation's Children's Fund (UNICEF)

In the News

Australia Joins Vietnam War.

The Ikeya-Seki comet is discovered by two Japanese astronomers during September.

Pope Paul VI becomes the first Pope to visit the United States.

Great Train Robber Ronnie Biggs escapes from Wandsworth Prison and flees to Brazil.

Malcolm X shot in New York.

70 mph speed limit imposed on British roads.

Ranger 9 sends back live TV broadcast when it crashes on to the moon.

Popular Films - Mary Poppins, The Sound of Music, Goldfinger, My Fair Lady.

The Mini Skirt appears in London.

The Post Office Tower opens in London.

The Maple leaf becomes Canada's new national flag symbol.

1965 Calendar.

January 1965
Sun	Mon	Tue	Wed	Thu	Fri	Sat
					1	2
3	4	5	6	7	8	9
10	11	12	13	14	15	16
17	18	19	20	21	22	23
24	25	26	27	28	29	30
31						

February 1965
Sun	Mon	Tue	Wed	Thu	Fri	Sat
	1	2	3	4	5	6
7	8	9	10	11	12	13
14	15	16	17	18	19	20
21	22	23	24	25	26	27
28						

March 1965
Sun	Mon	Tue	Wed	Thu	Fri	Sat
	1	2	3	4	5	6
7	8	9	10	11	12	13
14	15	16	17	18	19	20
21	22	23	24	25	26	27
28	29	30	31			

April 1965
Sun	Mon	Tue	Wed	Thu	Fri	Sat
				1	2	3
4	5	6	7	8	9	10
11	12	13	14	15	16	17
18	19	20	21	22	23	24
25	26	27	28	29	30	

May 1965
Sun	Mon	Tue	Wed	Thu	Fri	Sat
						1
2	3	4	5	6	7	8
9	10	11	12	13	14	15
16	17	18	19	20	21	22
23	24	25	26	27	28	29
30	31					

June 1965
Sun	Mon	Tue	Wed	Thu	Fri	Sat
		1	2	3	4	5
6	7	8	9	10	11	12
13	14	15	16	17	18	19
20	21	22	23	24	25	26
27	28	29	30			

July 1965
Sun	Mon	Tue	Wed	Thu	Fri	Sat
				1	2	3
4	5	6	7	8	9	10
11	12	13	14	15	16	17
18	19	20	21	22	23	24
25	26	27	28	29	30	31

August 1965
Sun	Mon	Tue	Wed	Thu	Fri	Sat
1	2	3	4	5	6	7
8	9	10	11	12	13	14
15	16	17	18	19	20	21
22	23	24	25	26	27	28
29	30	31				

September 1965
Sun	Mon	Tue	Wed	Thu	Fri	Sat
			1	2	3	4
5	6	7	8	9	10	11
12	13	14	15	16	17	18
19	20	21	22	23	24	25
26	27	28	29	30		

October 1965
Sun	Mon	Tue	Wed	Thu	Fri	Sat
					1	2
3	4	5	6	7	8	9
10	11	12	13	14	15	16
17	18	19	20	21	22	23
24	25	26	27	28	29	30
31						

November 1965
Sun	Mon	Tue	Wed	Thu	Fri	Sat
	1	2	3	4	5	6
7	8	9	10	11	12	13
14	15	16	17	18	19	20
21	22	23	24	25	26	27
28	29	30				

December 1965
Sun	Mon	Tue	Wed	Thu	Fri	Sat
			1	2	3	4
5	6	7	8	9	10	11
12	13	14	15	16	17	18
19	20	21	22	23	24	25
26	27	28	29	30	31	

www.ingramcontent.com/pod-product-compliance
Lightning Source LLC
Chambersburg PA
CBHW071238280526
45787CB00002B/985